Looking For A New England

Selected Poems

Djenane Watkins

ISBN – 13: 978 – 1523856251
ISBN – 10: 1523856254

Craig,

For 'keeping the
Feast'! 2015-2016.

Djerare

FOR MY GRANDCHILDREN

Claudie, Antonia, Elliott, Theo
and Leo

CONTENTS

ACKNOWLEDGMENTS

Grateful thanks go to Sally Lewis and Marjorie Wilson for breathing life into these poems, to Sue Wilkinson for all her help over the years, and to Judy Turner and my husband Geoff, for their unflagging support.

immigrant

Today I have been annoyed by a waitress;
She has unleashed a large stray apostrophe
Before a small and unsuspecting s,
Upon the blackboard in the cheap café.
I want to thrust an eraser into her plump hand,
But then I would have to make her understand
That I too am misplaced,
I also am displaced.
And yet I speak her language better than she,
I have a choice palette of words to beg and plea,
And I can punctuate for England.
I know her history, her kings and queens,
As well as I know my own dreams.
I know how many layers to stave off the cold,
I've learnt to drink and curse the old.
I can form an orderly queue when ordered to,
Mind my p's and q's and say how do you do,
As I offer a shaking quivering hand,
But how do I make her understand
That like the apostrophe before the s,
I am the diaspora,
I am the dispossessed.

new girl

That new girl needs teaching a lesson they said,
We'll learn ye, they said, and they did.
We'll learn ye so you never come back for more,
We'll learn ye what this school is for.

Geography's first lesson today, there's a dead nice town
Right over the other side of the playground,
A nice quiet town, you'll like it there,
No one shouts and no one swears,
You can shout all you like, no one'll care;
It's called Coventry, and we're sending you there.

Next lesson's sums, it's simple, there's five of us,
There's one of you, you're what's called sur-plus,
Six is a number that's never allowed,
Five is a gang, six is a crowd.

If I put my hand up they called me a swat,
They called me thick when I did not,
When the teacher asked was I alright,
They smiled, sweetness and light,
Told her not to worry, they'd make sure
To teach me what school was for.

It's been half a century, fifty years since then,
Since a plump pigtailed girl of ten
Stood in a playground on her own;
The new girl inside me has never gone.

cyberlove

Come to me by email, come to me by text,
Come to me by moonlight, whatever cybertime suits best,
Let me read your need for me on Facebook,
Skype me a longing loving look.

Let us gather up an apple, let us pick a blackberry,
Let us tweet and twitter like captive birds set free,
Think of every way to woo me, they'll soon invent some more,
Think of every way to woo me; just don't come to my door.

dissecting table

Unknown to any agency of cruelty or crime,
Four women, of any age, of any time.
Set before them a table of tempting treats,
In deference to diets, some light but luscious eats,
A bottle or two (as if one would do!)
Of pinot, and finally a select few
Exemplars of our popular press
Of the less discerning kind,
(Is there any other, never mind)
Allow some minutes for pleasantries to break the ice,
New hair, new teeth, new lover, how very very nice.
Now let their eyes fall to the table,
Each getting word in when they are able.
In seconds the Beckhams are divorced, how sad,
And what strange fate has befallen Brad.
Madonna's adopted from outer space,
They've plotted and planned the disgrace
Of almost the entire human race.

But that was the appetiser, the starter to the meal,
The main course has a closer feel.
Did you know so and so's husband is being shagged
By what's she called,
And thingamajig's husband can't be fagged
To shag at all,
Well now we've heard it all!
Not quite, there's more, as they devour in glee
The titbits from the telltale tree,
The tree they shake so fierce, so hard
Its fruit falls bruised and battered to the ground,
They on their knees then sniff like truffle dogs
Licking every last morsel with tired tongues.

Then, every bone of scandal picked, they say
Delightful, same time next week, same day.
Wonderful to see you everyone,
To have such friends to rely upon.

fragile

You have broken my life -
Or was it me, maybe, I dare say,
Being inclined to be clumsy that way.
Anyway, whatever,
Now it's lying at my feet
In shards shaped and sharp as old wives' tongues,
My toes bloody from prodding
Pieces closer.
If I kneel my knees will also bleed.
I need to kneel
To see what I can find,
Losers keepers, finders weepers.
I see a tiny cross,
Kiss or sacrifice I cannot tell,
Or perhaps it marks the spot
Of some small moment's hell.

wrong

Once I forgot and said 'dad, at school today I got'…
A silence loud as thunder to a child
Filled the air before he cried
Of what was I thinking, did I not care,
Was I at heart a Secondary Modern girl
With no regard for grammar after all,
Had I not been taught
To speak as one ought?

A skirt too tight, a heel too high,
A failure to look him in the eye,
A pop song playing on the radio,
God forbid I should offend him so.
Once a lipstick trace,
A hint of blusher on my face,
I even dared mention a boy in my school,
Ridiculous reckless unthinking fool.
I remember I yawned or must have looked bored,
He was not used to being ignored
By a sullen girl who had no manners
And no respect for her elders and betters.

A girl with an attitude,
No ounce of gratitude,
The way that youth has gone astray,
Yesterday's values thrown away.
I almost forgot what I wanted to say,
Yes dad I got, I received, achieved
Ten out of ten in my test today.

visitors

Home from school; there they were, it seemed that they were everywhere
Filling every sofa, every chair;
The twiggy spindly spidery spinstery ones,
The abundant overflowing overpowering ones,
Devouring genteel sandwiches and a sip
Of tea, but the scandal and the gossip,
How they devoured that.
I watched fascinated as in chorus each mouth,
Unencumbered by questions of truth,
Snapped shut, a red letterbox devouring morsels
Of lies wrapped up in bitesized parcels.
On they sat, what sights they were, what frights,
Corsets and thousand denier tights.
Nothing sacred, nothing safe,
No wonder no one wanted to be the first to leave.
Those women; how did they dare to breathe?
How could they bear to bleed?
At least they didn't care to breed.

women who wait

This is what we do, while we wait for you,
We who play the waiting game,
We count cars. After number seventeen you'll come.
With flowers. And on your knees.
That puppy look. Forgive me please.
This is what we do, while we wait for you,
A little more powder to the face,
Asking the mirror if every hair's in place,
Picture you dead, concussed, amnesiac
Never finding your way back.
In the ten long years each hour can seem
We're pathetic, we Penelopes, who dream
Of a moment framed by an ancient door,
When all will be as it was before.

the one at the back

She sits alone, the one at the back,
Discreet, apart, in shades of black.
A veil upon her feelings and her face,
A little lost, a little out of place.
She hears them whisper
Though they cannot, dare not whisper here.
It's her, is it her, is that really her,
Though they dare not, cannot whisper here.
She hears them all the same,
She hears them call her name.

And later they will say
They did not know her,
Did not notice her,
If it was her, was it her, was it really her,
Should she be there, should she not be there,
Later they will confer,
Though they did not notice her,
Did not know her.

Didn't notice her leave, did not see,
But still sighed their relief,
Though they dare not, cannot sigh here.

She hears them all the same,
She hears them call her name,
As a little early, a little late she leaves.
Leave her alone, let her be,
Let her go, she also grieves.

teenage dad

He got over it when she told him.
After all he was almost a man,
A real man, a proper man it seemed.
No worries he said, he had a plan;
He had a plan, she had a dream.

They'd get a flat, he'd find some work to do,
Saturday nights out with the lads, a pint or two,
He'd let her go out with her mates now and again.
Once a year they'd go to Spain.
He'd heard Lloret was very nice,
His mam and her boyfriend had been there
Once or twice.

They'd be alright, they had each other,
They'd be together, for ever and ever.
They had to be, it was on his tattoo,
And tattoos are painful things to undo.
Lucky he had a plan, a scheme.
He had a tattoo, she had a dream.

war bride

War doesn't only kill,
It marries and it marries ill.
My mother was just such a bride.
Handsome sailor filled with pride
At this exotic prize , this Egyptian queen,
Sent for her then, shipped her home
Like a lion's head, a trophy for his bed.
She flattered at this high command,
Left mother, father, familiar land,
Began a bruised and beaten life
In exile, a captive wife.
People spoke in tongues or so it seemed
And the love of which she'd dreamed
Was suddenly so small a thing,
As small tightbonding as a wedding ring,
Compared with how to ask for food
Or friends or help or home
Or tissues for the homesick tears
That flowed the long and lonely years.

don't blame the boys

It is not the child that is stubborn, only the sprout
That will not lift itself from the plate,
Only the peas that promise to stick in the throat,
Only the promise to behave and the sorry word,
That refuse to let themselves be heard,
Pronouncing letters so that the wrong sounds come out,
As if I care, it's not my fault.

Don't blame the man, the girl was gagging for it.
Don't blame the man, the child was asking to be hit.

Blame the bomb, round bellied, pregnant with so much death,
That fights its own way, fully formed, out of the earth.
Blame gravity as it hurls itself towards its grave,
Don't blame the master, blame the slave,
Blame anything, the weather, season or the time,
Just not the man, how could it possibly be him,
Don't blame the men, how could it possibly be them?

social divide

I thought the social divide
Was like the other one,
The north south divide
A figure of speech
A figure of fun.

I was wrong, I was wrong,
It's big and black and thick and long.
It's painted by the devil
And has a sign to say
Cross this at your peril,
I saw it clearly, I saw it today.

I saw a black eyed girl beside the road,
Clutching a single rose to sell,
She reached her arm out to the car
In hope but I could tell
The driver was too frightened of the line,
Drove off, saved himself in time.

I saw the vendor shivering outside the shop,
Passersby too cold too scared to stop,
To step over the line in case of bears or flees,
Or catching some dreaded exotic disease.
If they prick him he will not bleed,
But disappear, take his pain, his need
From sight, from mind,
As they mind the line,
How we must mind the line.

discovery

A girl at school said she was adopted
We reassured her, said what of it?
The sister of another
Turned out to be her mother,
Another girl again
Had a mother who was a man.

So why did they all turn against me
When I mentioned my discovery?
That I was Jewish, was that so bad?
They looked at me, how they looked,
As if I were completely mad.

I was a child, knowing nothing of time and tide,
How could I know when Jesus died.
I thought it was probably before the wars
And the bible didn't mention dinosaurs.
But there was a cross, so maybe I was there;
I was my mother's cross to bear.

The girls looked at me, at each other and talked,
Decided it may not have been my fault
That Jesus died.
But still I was like them, they said
And turned away
And the playground became my Calvary.

I looked at my hands, my nails, my feet
In my side a pain, could almost feel it bleed.
Was it by my hand, my nails, that Jesus died?
So thought the child
Was it for me that He was crucified?

the past

Even Jane Doe has a place to go,
Someone will lift her with their hands,
Caring or capable
Onto a slab.
How can a child understand
The taxi ride at midnight
Screaming for her father
The car in the blackness taking her further
Still screaming
Till the unsmiling landlady bids her hush,
Gives her a small square of paper to flush
The toilet and the tears;
Year after year after year
Why does fear
Still cling in the air
I was too afraid to breathe.

Silence dressed in its Sunday best,
The pipe trembling too much to light,
Time taking its time on its day of rest,
A child out of mind, out of sight.

If the black cat crosses in front of the house,
If I sit still and quiet as a mouse,
Maybe he won't shout quite so loud
Or so long.

If I wait till six before I breathe or speak,
Still as a mouse without a squeak,
Maybe his mood will lift, will pass
At last

And we can listen to Sing Something Simple,
He'll chuckle at an odd Black and White Minstrel,
It will be over
For now.

If she doesn't mention the war,
Or why or how or what was it for,
Then maybe the black miasma
That chokes the child
Will leave the room.
I lied
The black miasma
Has never left the room.

love in high heels

See her stumbling towards you
In her high high heels
Arms outstretched like a toddler
Hold out your hands
You can catch her
Feel her tumbling locks on your bare skin
The shoes don't fit that well
She could barely tell
So high and flushed from shopping
Then in the shoe shop dropping
Laughing into a chair
Took just about the first pair
Could just about see them
Through her tumbling hair.
Now here she is in front of you
Shoes cheap, shining, high and new.
Teetering, tottering,
This is how love feels,
Love stumbling towards you
In high heels.

baby boomers

Not for us walking out with sweethearts
Under a chaperone of stars.
For us acrobatic fumbling
In sweat and smoke filled cars.
Aromatic with cider and silk cut.

How could the living not stop the dying;
Kings and the common man.
Memphis and Vietnam.

And so we screwed and marched and schemed
And painted flowers on our face,
Immortal petals that we dreamed
Would save the human race.

And the babies came instead of bombs,
Babies dressed in dark grey suits,
Who tore the flowers from our hair,
Forging their future with stock and share.

On Facebook they discuss this dying breed
How quaint we were, how sweet, naïve,
Googling meanings for love hope and peace
The world's moved on, they sigh, relieved.

german lesson, 1965

She, armed with a degree and German dictionary,
Enters the battlefield gamely, if a little wary,
Equipped as ill as any soldier in Iraq,
We, forewarned, better ready to attack.

She, endowed with more than her fair share
Of comely brachial and facial hair,
Tight skirt bulging round enormous thighs,
Ladders long enough to take Jacob to the skies,
We ill concealing our teenage transport of mirth
At this gift of such pungent perspiring girth.

The first mistake, heaven sent; she turns her back!
We will, in our sweet way, make our attack.
The choreography is divine, a simple plan,
Each desk lid opens, and to a man
We remove our third of a pint and slurp
And slurp; and with our straws
Compete to make the loudest noise,
The crescendo; one almighty burp.

She, fleeing the room, curses the youth of today,
Curses education's lamentable decay,
'Twas ever thus, I hear you say,
It was so then, is so today.

war

War is an old man now, let's lay him to rest
Watch his painful shuffle, his shabby dress.
Once he had fine armour, now its sticks and stones,
Let's find a safe place for his broken bones.

Poor old war, his sight is failing, his eyes are sore,
He can't see where he's going any more
What use is he with a white stick in his hand
Lashing out anywhere, killing the best he can.

Poor old war, his hearing's not so good,
A million marched, yet he understood
Nothing of the shouting, nothing of the tears
What can you expect with his advancing years ?

His other senses aren't too hot
He's out of touch and can't smell the rot
Of burning broken flesh, a child's decay,
As for taste, he never had that anyway.

Poor old war, its time he retired, stepped down,
Gave up his rule, passed peace the crown.

small things lost

I wander the topography of my loss,
And ponder my shrinking geography, count its cost.
So many streets, the ones we walked the most,
The ones I cannot walk without your ghost.
And from our chip shop the warm familiar smell
Draws from me such grief as from the well
Where the Danaids drew water for their tears.
I've changed my scent, my hair, the clothes I wear,
The essence of me must surely shortly disappear.
I find myself outside the bakery
Where the croissants we used to eat
Were our Saturday morning treat,
The things we used to love the most,
The things I cannot eat without your ghost.
And on it goes, the songs I cannot hear,
Small talk and laughter I cannot bear,
Too much interest due on my account,
Losses mounting to such a large amount
I will never be in credit
Only in deficit
Of you.

abuse

The man who broke her childhood until it bled
Was a nice man a very nice man, they said.
I'd trust him with my life, I'm good at judging character.
I'd trust him with my wife, he'd never look at her.
They joked and laughed, cracked open a can
And left her with a lovely man.

He spun his patter, he was bored, misunderstood
It didn't matter, she shouldn't bother her pretty head,
He was only after comfort, closeness, he had such need
But hearts aren't the only things that bleed.

He took her gently , he took such care,
He didn't mean to hurt, hadn't meant to scare.
She was a brave girl, sweet and good as gold,
A man liked a girl who did as she was told.

Just one more thing, no need to name and shame,
Let's just keep this our little game,
We're partners in this innocent crime,
Keep our secret safe, see you next time.

letter

My grandmother died; distant lady, old, distant land.
A letter arrived; came from a careless postman's hand
Marked airmail.
Came home from school, my mother had cried a day away,
A lifetime away, a thousand miles away.
I hadn't understood how death could come
Through a door to a woman sitting alone.
Hid every letter after that; as if I could be a doorstop to death,
To a daughter's grief.
If I could I would have stood all day
My back against the shaft
That I could have kept at bay
That deadly draft.
All I have to fear today are bills,
Advertisements for viagra pills
And catalogues
Of clothes, causes and catastrophes,
Letters telling me people have died
Letters I still want to hide.

friends

Three friends, Jennifer and Josephine and Jacqueline,
Beauties to grace any fashion scene -
Fashion, they coyly whispered,
Was their passion.
Tiny patent leather shoes on narrow feet,
Shawls, bonnets, hair trim and neat,
Upturned noses snubbing the world,
Unbroken, unspoilt, my three girls.
Eyelashes thick, framing each wide eye,
That looked for the world about to cry.
Jennifer of the three the beauty queen,
Arrogant, aloof, ever so slightly mean,
Josephine my rock, calm and serene,
Jacqueline though more the drama queen,
Pouting lips, tears just in place
To make her point, not spoil her face.
I loved them all, they were the world to me
Jennifer and Josephine and Jacqueline
My friends, my dolls, my make believe,
So much the better, I knew they'd never leave.

dancers

Inside the fat girl, a thin girl.
Like Russian dolls two girls
Together in embrace of pirouettes and twirls
Thin girl delicate on slender points,
Fat girl creaking in her joints,
Thin girl spinning dizzily around,
Fat girl falling to the ground,
Head and heart pounding,
Head and heart breaking,
Fat girl's bulging tutu hiding dreams
Of a willowy girl in a garden,
Covent Garden,
Garlands
Of flowers at her feet.
And the silver necked swan inside her
Inclining gently full of grace
Towards the rapturous face
Of the standing crowd,
How proud
The fat girl was, filled with pride
For the thin girl inside.

a child crying

An ordinary day
In an ordinary café,
Muted sounds of cutlery and cruelty
And condolence.
Then a child howled,
A sound
Between a tantrum and a tragedy.
And into the vortex of its small being
Were sucked and siphoned
All our sorrows,
As if the child broke its heart for us all,
For all the tomorrows
We will never see,
All we might have been and now will never be.
The tears convention forbade us cry
Were transfused into its shaking frame,
The child cried for us and sucked us dry.

accident

I wanted so much to be wrong
But the two of them lingered just too long
On the road,
Too long for love, too long for life,
And knowing in my mind,
Looking in the mirror
I found what I had to find,
Such a surrender of white feathers filled the sky,
A snow of submission
Floating in white grief from heaven.
I drove on,
The doves who died for love I sang
The childish mantra filling my mind,
On the road, the death I left behind.

before you leave

Before you leave
I prepare to grieve
So the grieving's done
Before the day
You say will never come.
Before you go
I need to know
How I will survive
Even live
As I am told is the manner
Of the thing
When all I am missing
Is a man
Merely a man.

I build my battlements upon the shore,
Call in every metaphor
Of protection against mischance, mishap.
I prepare for your loss as I prepare for winter;
But who can be ready for such a cold snap?

dust

How is it that I shed my skin but not its memory?
It has no understanding of dementia
Or the demise of longing.
The skin I shed daily is now dust,
Your touch helped make it so.
I see the motes of our
Loving,
Touch the particles that were you and I
Suspended finely beneath the skylight
On this late summer's day.
At ten o'clock the cleaner comes
To sweep them away,
The end of the evidence
Of our decadence
Of our decay.

bnp

Only a million they tell me, such a small amount,
Tiny proportion, hardly worth the count,
Did much worse than they'd expected,
Far worse than pundits had projected.
That's OK then, we can relax, be at ease,
No danger from that particular disease.
But picture two million shoes marching to the polls,
A million hearts, a million souls.
A million ballot papers, isn't that a tree?
I wonder what kind of tree that would be,
Tree of evil with fruit of foul rank smell,
Roots grubbing down to the very bowels of hell.

flies

Having buzzed briefly as scandal
And sated with the power to irritate
They lie now still
On floor and chair and windowsill
And await their ceremony.
The others watch from behind the curtain,
As if perhaps they expect a miracle still.
Don't they know that to cleanly kill
Is our species' own and special skill.

why

If only stupid people were right.
If only fortune cookies told the truth.
The lady on the pier told me I'd lead a life of glorious
Danger
Marry a tall dark handsome stranger
Find romance
Fat chance.
If only they were right,
The holocaust deniers
Purveyors of happy lies.
But the good people,
Doctors,
And those who knock at the door
Somewhere between the hours of three and four,
They are never wrong
Though they must long to be,
Bringing a truth that no one can bear
In their overcoats and sensible shoes,
Bringing a truth no one wants to hear
Why do good people bring bad news?

words

Words are where you hide,
I close my eyes and count to ten
And shout ready or not
I'm coming in.
I look first in the thicket
Of your words of love
To see if you are lying there,
You are not
Nor in the forget me not
Of promises
And undeleted messages.
I look next in the reeds and weeds of wasted words,
Where last I caught you lying,
Still no sign.
There you are at last,
In those words you threw away when leaving,
Cast aside like an old sock,
The last place I thought to look.

garden centre

Can anything bring greater grief to the tormented
Than words, when overheard, of those contented
With gods more biddable and more cheaply bought.
Garden centres are the place; how I envy those
Who find their solace in a crocus or a rose.
I watch and try to copy, mimic them,
As they feel, discuss, dissect each stem
And leaf and flower, then choose and pay
And satisfied head for the café,
Congratulate themselves in unity of voice
Upon the wisdom of their choice.
I want to be as they are, but cannot,
Camouflaged, disguised, I hope that they can't spot
That I am of another species, a different plant,
Aloof, exotic, arrogant,
Hands hardened by a different toil,
Transplanted from a distant soil,
Where I grow words instead of weeds,
Where birds of prey peck at seeds
Of thought,
Until the land is barren, the ground is bare
And nothing grows except despair.

patience

Worth the winter for the damsel's lace,
Worth the waiting for the miracle
Of small feet and hands and face,
For memory to fade and pain to make the pearl
Or pass,
For an innocence of snowdrops to come
At last.
Patient as Penelope as she
Stitched up time,
As Job comforted in the long silence.
How hard it is not to tear the string
Till fingers bleed,
Patience wearing thin,
Waiting for it to end,
Waiting for it to begin.

the annoyance of love

You take up more and more and too much and far too much
Heartspace.
A heart as tight as Tesco's on Saturdays, no place
For old ladies and starving children and silly soap stars dying, no
place for me. How lost I am;
Thank God for instinct and sat nav.
I have taken so many wrong turnings,
You think I mean metaphorically,
No, I mean literally,
Really, actually
Maddeningly.
And yet people in love must run their empires
As if sober; small worlds
Of eager boys and typing girls,
No wonder the country's in a mess,
Perhaps we need to love a little less.

telephone

Confound the damned insufferable thing,
As if by its refusal to ring
It takes your part.
Sticks and stones may break the bones,
But silence breaks the heart.
And when the silence breaks what then?
Calcutta calling
Or manna falling from the skies,
Holidays won, kitchens, cars,
Men peddling every manner of lies,
Long lost cousins from abroad,
Aunts I'd long thought dead.
I kill them now and almost want the silence
I had come to dread.
It comes again, tears me apart,
Sticks and stones may break the bones,
But silence breaks the heart.

no wonder

No wonder hearts attack;
So much hurt held hostage for so long,
How can such pain belong
In such a small and sacred space.

No wonder hearts break:
Who could take such endless beating,
And all for such a fleeting
Eternity of embrace.

But what rebellious hearts we have,
Who take us prisoner to the grave;
They beat and bleed and love and hate,
And skip and leap without a by your leave.

But remember, remember please,
When this heart of mine is still,
Striking unto death against my will,
Remember, remember please,
How you were always my heartsease,
How you are always my rest in peace.

ABOUT THE AUTHOR

Djenane was born in Weymouth and read French and German Combined Honours at Birmingham University. She taught Modern Languages, English, Drama and Latin for forty years and is now retired.

She has written and directed numerous award winning one act plays for both adults and children as well as two pantomimes. In 2010 she founded a small independent drama company, The Valley Players.

Djenane has three children and five grandchildren and lives in North Yorkshire with her husband.

Printed in Poland
by Amazon Fulfillment
Poland Sp. z o.o., Wrocław